Colouring
Birds

OVER 40 DELIGHTFUL PICTURES
WITH FULL COLOURING GUIDES

ARCTURUS

ARCTURUS

This edition published in 2015 by Arcturus Publishing Limited
26/27 Bickels Yard, 151–153 Bermondsey Street,
London SE1 3HA

ISBN: 978-1-78212-871-7
AD003897UK

Printed in China

Introduction

Birds have always been a source of fascination for many people – not only naturalists, but also those of us who just like to set up a bird table in the garden so we can watch their activities and admire their beauty. They are wonderful subjects to paint and draw, too, but difficult if you are not an experienced artist. You can photograph birds so you can study them at leisure, but finding out how to portray feathers and colours so that you can make them come alive on paper is another matter.

The answer is to learn from artists of the past, discovering how they captured the essence of the birds they painted. The plates in this book are taken from *A History of the Birds of Europe* (1871) by H E Dresser and *The Birds of America (1840–44)* by John T Bowen and John James Audubon. In the days before photography came of age, accurate, detailed paintings were the only way of providing a visual record of a species – but the artistry of Audubon's work rose far above a careful depiction of the subject for the benefit of scientists and appealed to the general public curious to know about the natural world.

Audubon often worked with watercolour, combining it with pastel to render the texture of feathers. You may find it easiest to start with coloured pencils, though. By blending them you will be able to achieve the rich colours of the plates – but take care to follow the direction of the feathers as you work. For watercolour, you need only a small set of paints and a watercolour brush with a fine point – a No. 6 round brush is a good size to begin with. Thus equipped, you're ready to go. The delight of a colouring-in book is that you can get straight into applying colours without worrying about your drawing skills, safe in the knowledge that the outlines and features of your birds will look true to life.

Diana Vowles

Key: List of plates

1 Firecrest *(Regulus ignicapillus)* and goldcrest *(Regulus regulus)*

2 Waxwing *(Bombycilla garrulus)*

3 Western bluebird *(Sialia mexicana)*

4 Harris's buzzard, or Harris's hawk *(Parabuteo unicinctus)*

5 Common redstart *(Phoenicurus phoenicurus)*

6. Common kingfisher *(Alcedo atthis)*

7 Golden oriole *(Oriolus oriolus)*

8 Azure-winged magpie *(Cyanopica cyanus)*

9 Eagle owl *(Bubo bubo)*

10 Red-rumped swallow *(Cecropis daurica)*

11 Dalmatian pelican *(Pelicanus crispus)*

12 Black-headed bunting *(Emberiza melanocephala)*

13 Rose-coloured starling
(Pastor roseus)

14 Lazuli Bunting
(Passerina amoena)

15 Common redpoll
(Carduelis flammea)

16 Pine grosbeak
(Pinicola enucleator)

17 Griffon vulture
(Gyps fulvus)

18 Northern cardinal
(Cardinalis cardinalis)

19 Greater flamingo
(Phoenicopterus roseus)

20 Common buttonquail
(Turnix sylvaticus)

21 Two-barred crossbill *(Loxia leucoptera bifasciata)* and white-winged crossbill *(Loxia leucoptera leucoptera)*

22 Swallow-tailed flycatcher or scissor-tailed Flycatcher *(Tyrannus forficatus)*

23 Common kestrel
(Falco tinnunculus)

24 Northern bullfinch
(Pyrrhula pyrrhula pyrrhula)

25 American goldfinch
(Spinus tristis)

26 Brandt's Jay
(Garrulus glandarius brandti)

27 Townsend's warbler
(Setophaga townsendi)

28 Common starling
(Sturnus vulgaris)

29 Long-eared owl
(Asio otus)

30 Steller's jay
(Cyanocitta stelleri)

31 Purple heron
(Ardea purpurea)

32 White-throated Kingfisher
(Halcyon smyrnensis)

33 Hawfinch
(Coccothraustes coccothraustes)

34 Green woodpecker
(Picus viridis)

35 Golden-winged warbler
(Vermivora chrysoptera)

36 Red-backed shrike
(Lanius collurio)

37 Double-crested cormorant
(Phalacrocorax auritus)

38 Common wood pigeon
(Columba palumbus)

39 White-backed
woodpecker
(Dendrocopos leucotos)

40 Green-backed purple
gallinule *(Porphyrio
smaragdonotus)*

41 Scarlet tanager
(Piranga olivacea)

42 Caucasian great rosefinch
(Carpodacus rubicilla)

43 Savannah sparrow
*(Passerculus
sandwichensis)*

44 Greenfinch
(Carduelis chloris)

1

2

3

4

5

7

8

9

10

11

12

13

14

15

17

18

19

20

21

22

23

24

26

27

29

30

31

32

33

34

35

36

37

38

39

40

42

44